Million Dollar Man

Surviving Tuberculosis

Royce L. Gaye

Dedication

This book is dedicated to anyone who is battling, or overcame a life changing illness, especially Tuberculosis, at this time in your life. This also goes out to those with loved ones who are suffering, or who have suffered in the past. It is my sincerest hope that my story will inspire, motivate, and hopefully even entertain you while you are on this journey. I welcome you to laugh at my pain, and encourage you to find light in the midst of your own. Thank you for giving me the courage to share my story with you. Keep pushing, and God bless.

TABLE of CONTENTS

1

Chasing Hoop Dreams

I was just another aspiring athlete, working endlessly to pursue a lucrative basketball career. My hard work carried me through high school, and eventually landed me a full ride through college. I was determined to snag a contract, and provide for my family. Unfortunately, I was never drafted to an NBA team out of college as anticipated; but I was determined to make it happen by any means necessary. The next best thing was to pursue D-league, and other teams overseas. I worked out, and practiced frantically every single day. You could say I turned into a fanatic, waking up at 5am every morning to run 3 miles. I would return, eat breakfast, and head to the gym to hit weights, and then the basketball court afterwards. I put up at least 1000 shots on the court, 4 days out of the week. On the other days, I balled out in countless basketball games against other professional athletes at the Fonde Recreational Center in Houston, Texas. I would destroy these guys on the court every chance I got, trying to prove to myself and everyone else that I was as good as any; that I deserved it as much as they did.

I spent countless dollars of my own money, investing in myself, without the help of an agent. Imagine how tough that process was, being a young, hungry, determined guy fresh out of college. There was not a lot of money to work with, in between jobs, relying on the help of my family, and girlfriend (now wife) to get me through. They were all rooting for me, and held me down in every way possible. I attended D-league tryouts, as well as overseas tryouts in hopes of getting picked up. I thought I had finally got a break, when I landed a D-league contract with the Austin Toros. As with anything, it all boiled down to politics, and who you know. To my disappointment, I was not drafted yet once again. It was back to square one for me, but I refused to give up.

My funds started dwindling, so I picked up a temp gig to replenish the funds that were demolished attending these countless events.

About six months later, I received a random phone call. It was a recruiter scouting me for a select team to travel to India and showcase our skills. Ideally, it was supposed to land us a contract for one of Mumbai's professional teams. I was stoked for the opportunity, because not only was I hoping for a contract; the traveling experience was a huge blessing in itself! I scraped up the funds, packed my bags, and headed to India for 2 weeks, hoping to return (or not return) with a long-awaited contract.

When I arrived, the drama popped off from the jump! It was a complete disaster. There wasn't a recruiter or coach in sight to pick us up from the airport. We finally contacted someone who was able to come and transport us to the hotel. We were exhausted from the twenty plus hour flight prior, finally arrived to the hotel; and the culture shock began. My stomach was killing me, I had to take a HUGE dump, only to find that there wasn't a roll of toilet paper in sight! My only options were my hands, and a bidet sprayer to clean myself! I hunted down a manager requesting a roll of toilet paper, or some form of paper towels. I had never heard of this, and certainly wasn't accustomed to these practices. Somehow, the manager was able to round up some napkins; but I could already tell that I was in for a loooooong two weeks.

The next day, there was still no sign of

the coaches, and we had to immediately check out of the hotel, as that was not our final destination. We checked out, but had no transportation, so we were traveling on foot trying to find a bite to eat until they were able to get us a ride. We were in the slums of Mumbai, India. Like, the SLUM slums! As we were walking, we witnessed people urinating and taking a dump in the ditches, and might I remind you, THERE WAS NO TOILET PAPER IN SIGHT! I could feel myself turning into a complete germaphobe. I was praying that my bottle of sanitizer would somehow magically last me until my departure. My mind was blown, and at that point, I was terrified to eat, drink, or even close my eyes to go to sleep. I was rethinking the entire thing, maybe this was a big mistake!

We played about seven games during the course of that two weeks, made it all the way to the finals, and ultimately ended up losing the championship game. I felt alive on the court, fans were screaming my name and cheering for me, and even asking me for my autograph. I felt like THE MAN! It was an awesome feeling, and I couldn't help thinking, 'Please don't ask to shake my hand...but MAN! I could definitely get used to this!'. As the tournament came to a close, the coaches called us in individually to evaluate and discuss our performance, and future basketball career with the Mumbai teams. In my mind, I just knew I had killed it, ready to sign on the dotted line; but here we go once again. The B.S. began. The coach said to me, "Royce, you're a helluva a player; but I really don't think you would be a good fit for an India team. It seems to be too much of a cultural shock for you." He went on to say I complained about the food, the cooks preparing the meals with their bare hands, and just didn't feel that I would be happy out there long term. I debated with him about the things he was saying, knowing it was all true; but I knew he was already convinced, and his mind was already made up. Someone on my team had snitched to the coaches, and told them how I reacted to the cultural shock of being out there (and any remarks that I made regarding what we had witnessed and experienced). It was a dog-eat-dog world in the basketball arena; and someone took that opportunity to throw me under the bus. Now just for the record, India wasn't ALL bad. There were some nice parts in nearby areas, and we did have a good time sight-seeing, and collecting souvenirs to bring home to our families. It just wasn't anything I was accustomed to, and a whole new world from the United States.

I headed back home to Houston, disappointed and feeling like a failure once again. Three months went by when another opportunity presented itself for a top Mexican league, the LNBP. Someone came across a YouTube video of me, and wanted me to come to their tryouts. Fortunately, this time I didn't have to worry about a place to stay. The recruiter opened his home to me for the duration of my visit. I will admit, I initially thought it was all a big set-up, because the recruiter had no arms. Yes, I said NO ARMS. I remember thinking, how could he possibly help me? I know that sounds completely judgmental and stereotypical, but I'm only human. I thought, this must be a ploy to kidnap yet another American. With all my doubts and skepticisms, I took a huge leap of faith, and risked it all. After all, what else did I have to lose at this point? I was relentless, and giving up was never an option. Turns out, it was the best decision I could have made for myself at that time. The recruiter was legit, and one of the nicest guys I had ever met. He opened his home to me, fed me, showed me the city, and took me in as if I was one of his own. I didn't have to worry about a thing. After preparation and tryouts, all went well. I was finally offered a job, and was ready for takeoff. I was the second leading scorer of the team, and was named top player of the week on several occasions. The pay wasn't extravagant or enough to ball out, but it was a great start, and more than what I had coming in previously. All praises to the most High! My hard work was finally paying off, or so I thought.

I stayed in Mexico for eight months, having left my family, girlfriend, and entire life behind. As the season came to an end, I returned to my hometown, and began networking for the next big thing. I now had something solid on my resume, and expected greater opportunities. Six months went by with no feedback or opportunities, and I became very weary. I had to face reality, and it was time to get another job with a steady income. Bills had to be paid, and promises had been made. My lady had been patient long enough, after rocking with me for six years, and supporting my crazy ambitions. She was waiting on her ring, and it was time to deliver.

2

Settling Down

I landed a job finally, and started saving and replenishing my funds. While I did miss hooping, I was happy to finally get back to the money. Now I told you before, I had a promise to deliver on, and I had something very special in mind for my lady. It was a long time coming, but well worth the wait. I knew I should have done it sooner, but I didn't have the means to provide for her as a man should. As men (and especially young men), we always make the mistake of thinking we need to have it all together, and have lots of money before settling down. Instead, we should be settling down, and building together as a team. We always want to wait for the "right time" or the "perfect time"; but there is no such thing. You have to do what you can with what you have, and MAKE time for what's important in life.

It was time to officially take my queen off the market, despite not knowing what was next to come. I picked out a ring, and planned a proposal my lady would never forget. I splurged on her, got her hands and feet done, and took her on a shopping spree to pick out an outfit to wear out to dinner. Now we did have a slight problem; because I was not very clear on what exactly this shopping spree entailed. I mean she heard "shopping spree", and just lost her marbles! She wanted the outfit, shoes, and accessories too! I never said I would buy all of that! Needless to say, she was HOT! She was convinced that these items were all essential to completing her outfit; but I was on a budget. So, I made her put some stuff of the items back. I wanted to tell her, 'sorry babe, but all of my money went on this ring you about to get!'; but it would have ruined the surprise. She got over it eventually, and was able to pull off her ensemble (impressively so). It would be a dinner that would change her life, unbeknownst to her.

I asked for her dad's blessing, and was ready for take-off. I invited my close family and friends to dinner at the Cheesecake Factory in The Woodlands, and told everyone we would be celebrating a personal financial goal I had reached. After being seated on the patio, placing our orders, and mingling, I went into a speech on my sister bring a bouquet of fresh red roses from my car, and presented them to my beautiful queen, asking for her hand in marriage. I don't think I even need to tell you that of course, SHE SAID YES! Probably a HELL YES to be more exact, with an ABOUT DAMN TIME to add to it! It was an awesome (COLD) night to remember, filled with laughter, tears, photos and fun. Life was supposed to only go up from there.

3

Life Disrupted

A few months went by, and one day while working; I lifted a hefty sized box, and ultimately injured my back. I ended up taking a leave on Worker's Comp, getting X-rays and treatment from doctors. They were unable to diagnose anything, but the pain kept getting worse. Something was terribly wrong, and it was killing me to not have any answers on exactly what. My lower back would tighten up so bad I was unable to sleep at night. Most nights I had to sleep sitting up due to the severe sharp pains shooting up my back and discomfort. It was unlike any other pain I had ever experienced, and certainly did not feel like the normal sports' spasm I ever had before. Over time, the pain progressed, and my spine began curving to my left side, causing me to walk like an ole school pimp with a limp! My family and fiancé took notice, and started questioning what was going on with me. I threw money away seeing a chiropractor, thinking maybe I just needed some adjusting. He eventually suggested that I get an MRI done, because I was spinning my wheels by this time. Worker's Comp took forever ordering the MRI, but when they finally did, all hell broke loose.

Upon receiving the results from the MRI, they urged me to immediately get to the emergency room. They discovered a huge abscess on my spine. If you're unfamiliar with what an abscess is, it is a swollen area filled with pus. I rushed to the ER, and they performed a second MRI to confirm everything. They then took a sample of the pus from my back, and filled an entire testing tube. The pus was thick and yellow, and wasn't even close to being fully drained from my spine. The doctors decided that surgery needed to be performed immediately, still not knowing what was growing inside of my body at the time. They were more concerned with draining the abscess they had discovered. They put me under, and proceeded with cutting the abscess from out of my spine. I remained in the hospital recovering from the surgery for at least a week's length of time, with my fiancé by my side every step of the way. As I prepared to discharge from the hospital, the doctors diagnosed me with Tuberculosis based on their lab results. No big deal, that can be cured, were supposed to cure the disease, along with other antibiotics and pain meds post-surgery. They told me they would be in touch to follow up after further monitoring the growth of my lab specimens. Once I filled the prescriptions, I was blown away by the costs of all of the medications. Even with insurance, I had no idea how I was going to foot this pharmacy bill every week. The total was somewhere around three hundred dollars, and I immediately felt sick to my stomach. Here I was, with stitches in my back, fighting tuberculosis, and now having to worry about how I was going to pay to get cured! Lucky for me, I was soon able to get the medications from the health department. Whew! This lightened my load a lot, and my prayers had been answered. I was then assigned a caseworker, who would make visits to supervise me when taking the meds. I had to ensure I would be home at the times he would arrive, and I immediately began to feel like I was a stigma. Here I am, a grown man, having to be supervised while taking medications! It was a complete invasion of privacy, having this complete stranger coming into my home. As frustrating as it was, I was more than willing to do whatever it took to get cured. I took the medications faithfully, and within two months, my stitches began to heal. I went and had them removed, and was finally able to enjoy taking a shower again. I was growing highly impatient with all of those wipe offs. I recall one particular day, as I was enjoying a nice, steaming, hot shower, I stepped out to dry myself; and suddenly I felt a wet sticky feeling on my back where the surgical incision had been made. I thought, "what in the hell rushed downstairs, and asked my mom to check it out. She looked at it, and squeezed the incision where the pin sized hole was. Suddenly, the hole popped like a pimple, and begin oozing lots of pus. The closest thing my mom could grab to absorb the pus was a diaper that belonged to one of my little nephews. You would not believe how much pus was absorbed into that diaper! The diaper was soaked to capacity! It may sound extremely gross, but this is the honest truth. It was actually a blessing in disguise; because if the pus had not been released, where would it have manifested?? You guessed it! INSIDE OF MY BODY!

I immediately returned to the doctor the very next day, concerned and freaked out about the leakage I had experienced the day before. The doctor told me, "Oh, that's just fluid being released from the surgery". I remember thinking, this guy is a GOT DAMN LIE! There was NO WAY that was considered normal in my mind; but he was the expert, so I went with it. I had convinced myself that I was getting better, feeling very positive about my progress. That's just how I am, always seeing the glass half full. Relentless. Giving up is never an option.

A couple of days went by, and I received a dreadful phone call. More lab results were in, and they did not come bearing good news. They told me to immediately stop taking the prescribed TB meds, because they were not working. As it turned out, I did not just have Tuberculosis, I had Multiple DRUG Resistant Tuberculosis; also known as MDR.

such a thing! What this meant was, I had a form of TB that was resistant to treatment with two of the most effective and powerful first line of drugs. I was SHOOK, and it didn't stop there. They told me to pack my bags, and immediately head to the headquarters in San Antonio, Texas. Talk about LIFE DISRUPTED! While I was willing to do whatever it took to get well, I had no idea what kind of turn my life was really about to take. Here we were, in the midst of planning our wedding about forty plus days away, just settling into our new home; and now I was uprooted and summoned to another city, three and a half hours away. It was all like a bad dream, that I couldn't awake from.

4

Coming to Grips

It was a long, dreadful, lonely drive, just me, and a million crazy thoughts racing through my head. I was determined to stay positive; and on the bright side, at least I was finally going to be in the right hands. Upon checking in, I was immediately approached by the staff and doctors and escorted to a quarantine room. They grilled me with many questions regarding my background and travel during the intake process. Most importantly, they asked where I had traveled in the past; and lo and behold, both countries (India AND Mexico) were cited for being high risk of contracting Tuberculosis! The sad part is, I can't even begin to pinpoint when, where, and how I was exposed to the infectious disease. They started running bloodwork, and took another sample of fluid from my back. By this time, my surgical wound had gotten bigger due to the constant build-up of fluid. I had to do another MRI, and was then quarantined for twenty-one consecutive days. I had to stay in a confined room, and could only leave out with a mask on to go outside of the building. I was even prohibited from leaving the premises, all until the test results would consecutively come back negative. They had to be sure that I was not contagious. My wedding was still about forty-five days away, and now I wasn't even sure that I would be released in time to make it down the aisle. I explained to the doctors and staff that I was about to get married, but they said the only way I could get a pass was if all of my results came back normal. This added to my already heightened anxiety, but my fiancé and I remained prayerful and hopeful. Things were happening so fast, and I had no control of my fate. To add to the stress, the doctors bluntly told me that it was a strong possibility they would be unable to find the right combination of drugs to treat this rare form of TB, since it was highly resistant. Now I had to worry about if I might be planning my funeral soon instead of my wedding. I lived on pins and needles with each passing week, fingers crossed, praying for negative test results each time. The results continued to come back negative, meaning I was not contagious; after all, the TB was never in my lungs. One of the biggest misconceptions about Tuberculosis, is that it only gets in your lungs. This could not be farthest from the truth. You can get spine (which was shocking enough for me), but there were others in the hospital who had it in their brains, eyes, rectums, genital areas, and even their feet! It's a whole other world you know nothing about, or could even imagine.

During this dreadful time period, there was finally some light at the end of the tunnel. They were finally able to find a combination of drugs that my Tuberculosis would react to. This would be the first step towards getting cured. After the final week of quarantine, they were able to conclude that I was not contagious! All praises to God! My fiancé and I were relieved and overjoyed that we would not have to cancel our wedding after all!

Now this was only a tiny bit of relief, but I was still up for a long, hard road ahead. The doctors explained to me that I would be on these drugs for two years, seven days a week. I also had to get a painful butt injection five days a week. Now most people tell you that when you take medications, you can tell if they are working if your body starts feeling better. This was the complete opposite! Your body would feel worse as the medications are working in this case! There were also many side effects from all of these drugs, including psychological, loss of hearing, loss of eyesight, color blindness, nerve damage, and even kidney failure. I mean it was enough to make you LOSE YOUR MIND. At one point I thought, jumping off of a bridge or playing in traffic might feel better than this. I would never take my own life, but I can definitely say that the thought of it crossed my mind. People around me couldn't even begin to it look so easy. I make everything look so easy. So much so, that my family and friends didn't take my illness very serious. They SAID that they knew how serious it was with their mouths, but their actions showed me otherwise. I would still get dumb, trivial phone calls from my parents and sisters bickering, whining, and complaining about not getting their way with the wedding plans and festivities. My fiancé would complain and vent to me about things happening at work. It all seemed so petty and unimportant to me at that time. As a matter of fact, I WISHED I had their so-called problems they were complaining about!

Meanwhile, I was stuck miles away by myself, in a hospital where I felt completely out of place. I was surrounded by all kinds of crazy people:

alcoholics, drug addicts, prostitutes and bums! People I prided myself on staying the hell away from! Yet here we all were, stuck together, in the same lounge, hanging out and watching T.V., trying to get rid of the same disease! It was a harsh reality check. Just as death has no respect of persons, neither does having TB or any other illness. At this point, I was no better than they were; and in all honesty, I needed the interaction with them because they were the only ones that understood what I was going through.

The doctors and staff constantly came into my room disrupting my sleep, taking vitals, drawing my blood, and shoving pills down my throat. The irony here, is that they urge you to get "plenty of rest". That must be some kind of sick joke. I was in so much pain that sleep was no longer a luxury or relief. I simple tasks, like trying to stand up and sit down, or get in and out of bed. It hurt just to even sneeze or cough, or perform any activity that would tense up the back muscles. Talk about mind over matter. It was going to take lots of will power and determination to overcome this battle. I have a pretty high tolerance for pain, but THIS, was unlike anything I could have imagined.

The most recent MRI results finally came back, and the results did not look promising. There was a huge hole in the area where I had surgery, still unhealed, and leaking lots of fluid. It turns out, they should have never even performed the surgery in the first place. The abscess was never supposed to be cut open, because the right medications would have absorbed it eventually anyway. The surgeon had no idea, because he did not have the knowledge of a Tuberculosis specialist. Now, I am stuck with a large dent and scar in my back, because they didn't do enough research on how to treat me. I had to go and see a back specialist, to prepare me for the worst-case scenario. In the event that the medications didn't start working in a timely manner, they would have to go through my abdomen, and cut the rest of the infection eaten away on my spine. He was very graphic and blunt, and said, "Dude, I'm just gonna be honest with you. Your back looks like shit!" (as if I didn't already know this). He then went into this whole spill on how I may as well freeze some of my sperm, because it was a possibility that I would never be able to have kids. If he had to result to a second back surgery, it would leave me paralyzed

I could have caved this guy's face in! God was testing me in the worst way! I thought to myself THE DEVIL IS A LIAR! WHO THE HELL ARE YOU TO TELL ME I MIGHT NOT HAVE ANY KIDS?! It was praying time for sure! I wasn't going out without a fight, and this asshole wasn't about to determine my fate. I didn't hear anything else that came out of his mouth after that. Everything else he said fell on deaf ears. I'm so glad that I'm a strong willed and determined guy, not easily swayed or broken. When most people want to throw in the towel, I am fueled to go even harder. This was a lot to take in, but I am sure that God had a plan by taking me on this gruesome detour.

CHAPTER 5

Conquering the Big Day

The big day was now before us, and I was most excited about getting a break from the hospital scene. Since my results came back all good, I was granted the pass to return home for two weeks for the wedding. Of course, I still had an obligation to keep up with my treatment plan. It was literally NO days off. They sent medications home with me to cover the weekends when the clinic was closed. The other five days of the week, I had to drive to the clinic for my injections, and the other medications. To be completely honest, it was a real hassle. Yet and still it felt great to be home, was excitedly putting the finishing touches on our big day; so, I think she really forgot how I was feeling at the time. We were getting married come hell or high water, and I knew better than to get in her way! She asked me to do two things. I had to book the limo, and pick up my suit. Simple, right? I was FURIOUS! You would swear she asked me to build a bridge on a highway, but doing ANYTHING extra literally wore me out! It annoyed me that she even asked! I survived it, but boy she could have called the whole thing off and I wouldn't have even put up a fight! My groomsmen had NO chill, forcing me to go to the strip club to celebrate the night before the wedding. I mean, WHO DOES THAT?! I knew full well I wasn't up for that. I couldn't even fully enjoy myself. I was hurting, and couldn't even feel my feet due to having neuropathy from the intensity of the medications; but I guess I did what any guy would have done in my shoes. On second thought, I had to be out of my mind. That had to be one of the dumbest things I had ever done! I took one for the team though (as always) to make everyone else happy. They just wouldn't take no for an answer. They were popping bottles having a blast, and all I wanted to do was go to bed. I don't know why I didn't go with my first mind and pull a Houdini, but once again, I made it through.

I definitely paid for it on the day of the wedding. Thank GOD it was scheduled later in the evening. I wasn't hungover (because Lord knows I couldn't drink on all of those medications); but I was EXHAUSTED. I had a blast doing the photo shoot with my groomsmen early on, but I was tapped out before things even got started good. I tried to close father-in-law wouldn't let me make it. He saw me with my eyes closed, and still kept right on talking to me! In my mind I was saying, 'FATHER-IN-LAW, SHUT THE F- UP!', but I didn't want to hurt his feelings. That's my guy though, so I let him make it. It's like I said before, people don't care what you're going through. In my case, they couldn't see past my smile. I'm just laid back, light-hearted, funny guy, Royce; always smiling, even when it hurts. People saw me smiling, and forgot what I was battling, or just didn't quite take it seriously. There's an old saying, sometimes you have to laugh to keep from crying. I made pain look good.

Well, the queen and I made it down the aisle. Despite how I was feeling, I still had a great time. It was nobody but God that got me through that day. I was starving, feeling nauseous, and I began to get aggravated with people asking me to take a million pictures. My mom pissed me off during our dance, because she kept telling me to put some extra "UMPH" in my dance moves. My dad thought it was funny, and this pissed me off even more! She knew damn well my back was in pain, and my movements were limited! This was the same lady, that had just harassed my wife about getting a stool to stand on, so that I wouldn't hurt my back (bending down to kiss her at the altar)! Now you want me to kill myself dancing with you?! I was like DEAR GOD WHAT IS WRONG WITH THESE PEOPLE!??! That's my mom though; you gotta love her.

As the night came to an end, we rode off into the night relieved that it was all finally over. The limo driver chauffeured us around for the remainder of our home. My dad's birthday was the very next day, and good ole mom strikes again. She decided to throw an impromptu party for him at their house, on a MONDAY, and then guilt tripped me into attending. I told her I was tired and didn't feel like coming out. I mean after all; I DID just get married the night before. She just wouldn't take no for an answer. Just inconsiderate and disrespectful; but that's a whole other story for another day. My wife and I went ahead and attended the party. I was the one fighting TB, but making yet another sacrifice to keep others happy.

It was tough having to return to San Antonio after getting a little taste of normalcy and freedom; but I was a bit relieved I could finally get some much-needed rest (well, somewhat). My wife headed back with me for a few days once my two-week pass was up. I checked back into the hospital, and was able to get another pass for the weekend. We had gotten a hotel room a short distance away, just to relax and unwind from all of the activity. That was the closest we were able to get to a honeymoon after the wedding. We still haven't officially taken one to this very day; but it's definitely on my bucket list to make it up to her sometime soon.

Shortly after settling in from the wedding festivities, some other unwelcomed changes took place. My rear was beginning to lump up severely due to all of the constant injections. The only alternative was to insert a PICC line, medically known as a peripherally inserted central catheter. I be accomplished. Another traumatic and painful experience to add under my belt. The PICC line was dangerous, high maintenance, and itched like crazy! I mean it was just one torture after another! I had to constantly keep it cleaned, and ensure that no air bubbles were released into the tube. If air bubbles would have gotten inside of the PICC line, I wouldn't have even had to worry about the TB taking me out. Venous air embolism is NO JOKE!

I also had to be careful how I slept, because if you slept wrong on it you were liable to bleed out. One night, it almost happened to me. I accidentally slept on the side where the PICC line was inserted. I guess I may have applied too much pressure, because I woke up in a pool of blood the next morning. I almost had a heart attack from the shock of seeing it. I was blessed that the outcome

wasn't as bad as it could have been; but I felt like I

just couldn't catch a break.

6

Unforgettable Acquaintances

Remember when I said I was surrounded by all kinds of crazy people in this particular hospital? I promise you; they made this journey a heck of a lot easier as they became my daily source of entertainment. I won't say their real names in order to maintain confidentiality, but there was a particular patient who made his mark in my mind forever. Early one morning I awakened to the sounds of a loud, animated voice yelling down the hallway. "SA-LUUUUUUUUUEYYYY!!!!" is all I kept hearing, and I thought to myself, 'Oh my GOD I'm in the looney bin'! I didn't get out of the bed right away to see who it was; but I soon had my chance later that day as I left from my room to go and eat breakfast. I was walking down the hallway and I heard the same voice going on a rant. He was yelling at the nurses saying, "MAMA!!! I'M HUNGRY MAMA!! MY HEAD HURT MAMA! SALUUEYYY!!!". I finally came face to face with a short, middle-aged, Hispanic guy, approximately in his 50's. He had dark hair, beady eyes zoned out on meds, and a long, thick caterpillar shaped moustache almost covering his entire top lip. I could always hear his flip-flops scooting down the hallway. When I finally came face to face with him for the first time, I stopped, looked at him and said, "HEY! Stop making all that noise in the mornings man!" He looked back at me with those crazy beady eyes, and started firing off his rants with a slight growl! "SALUUEEEEYYY!!! SALUEEYY LA HOHO!! SALUEY LA FOFO!!" Whatever he could think of to say with "SALUEY", he yelled it out. I must have been crazy too, because I got quite a kick out of this guy. I looked forward to seeing him and hearing his rants. He would flirt with all of the nurses, yell out vulgarities, and

The funny thing was, the nurses thought they were giving him enough meds to calm him down, but it seemed as though they amped him up even more! My buddy had Tuberculosis in his brain, which is probably why he was a bit estranged and would go off the deep end at times. He wasn't entirely throwed off though, because he actually knew how to speak English, and would even have civilized conversations with me at times. I think his mind would come and go due to the intensive damage the infection had caused. I can say this though, when he discharged from the hospital, I experienced a great feeling of sadness and grief, because I knew that I would more than likely never see him again. He had become the highlight of my days; and I wish there was a way that I could have kept in contact with him and his family just to see how he was doing. Things were never the same after he left.

Another bond was formed through this journey, but we are fortunate enough to still be in contact to this day. My boy treatment was only supposed to last for eight months. Unfortunately, his stay was extended to four years. Aside from having Tuberculosis, V. also suffered with gout in his feet. Many patients suffered with health conditions prior to being diagnosed with TB. As a result, it would heighten the effects of any pre-existing health issues, meaning a higher intake of medications to deal with each and every one. We would all laugh at each other's pain, because we had to make light of our situations some kind of way. We would laugh at V. whenever his gout flared up, because it always looked like he was walking on eggshells (he would walk so carefully). Of course, he would clap right back and make fun of my crooked, limped to the side demeanor. His comeback would be, "that's why you walk like a two-dollar pimp with ya crooked ass! Where you going? To pimp some heaux!??"! I would then say, "Naw the only one I'm pimping is MY WIFE!"! It's a great feeling to be able to make light of a painful situation. Thank goodness there were a few other patients that shared my same journey. She was a patient as well, and they found comfort in each other along the way. They are now happily married, and back in the real world building a new life together.

The downside to this illness, is that everyone is not as fortunate to make it to discharge. There was one really nice lady I'll refer to as "Mimi". She was in a wheel chair with a feeding tube through her stomach. I remember her sharing that her infection was in the lungs, hips, and kidneys after spreading. She was there even before I was admitted. We all thought Mimi was getting better, and she went in for one last surgery on her hip before being released from the hospital. I never saw Mimi again, and after about two weeks had gone by, I noticed a large photo of her sitting by the television in the lounge. A memorial had never even dawned on me. I guess I wasn't in my right mind. I said to the nurse, "Hey, I see you guys have a picture of Mimi in the lounge. Is it to remember her after she discharged and went home??". The nurses then

Unfortunately, Mimi's surgery didn't go very well. She passed away on the operating table.". I suddenly felt sick in the pit of my stomach. I was more than shocked to say the least. Learning of that news really had me shook, but it was a real wake up call. That most definitely could have been me; but God saw fit for me to still be here. Not that I didn't know before, but in that instance, I knew just how short life really is. You can't take it for granted that you will always be around, or live to see another day. Whatever goals you have in life, don't put it off, or allow fear to stand in your way. You have to get out of your own way, and allow yourself to reach your fullest potential. Whatever beef you may have with your loved ones, won't matter once you are dead and gone. Love while you can; because our time is most definitely limited, so make it count.

7

The Road to Recovery

For the first year and four months, I would travel home on the weekends to be with my wife and family. This was a great outlet because I definitely needed the breaks away from the whole hospital scene. It was tough getting in and out of my car, and focusing on that road for three and a half hours. Also, I couldn't really feel the foot pedals due to the numbness in my feet. After a while, the medications also started to affect my vision. I started going color blind, and could hardly read the signs on the road. I barely made it that last an end. I panicked and started getting depressed at the idea of losing my sight. I was terrified out of my mind on that road with my eyes suddenly playing tricks on me. From that point on, my wife would come and pick me up, and take me back at the end of my visits.

So now, I can't feel my feet, I'm losing my vision, and still in pain, crooked to the side like Gumby. I was taking loads of pills to numb the pain, but they really weren't helping me at all. One day, I made a decision to stop taking all of the pain pills cold turkey. It was a waste of my time; so, I was going to tough it out. I went through a tough case of withdrawals, breaking out in cold sweats, and getting very irritable. I was so nauseous that I had to force myself to eat, but I knew I had to keep myself hydrated and nourished if I wanted to avoid sure you drink lots of water and keep those kidneys nice and moist! Get plenty of rest and have a healthy fatty diet!"

When you have TB, you have to consume a high fat diet because it causes you to lose a lot of weight. I was all for it because I was able to eat whatever I wanted, WHEN I wanted. My days and nights in the hospital consisted of ringing a bell asking for chocolate doughnuts, chips, cookies, and whatever else I craved that I could think of. To be honest, I was waited on hand and foot. I always like to turn the negative into a positive. So, in my mind, I was living like a king, and had servants catering to my every need! They would bring me food, wash my laundry, and chauffer me around to all of my appointments. My room was like a high-rise condominium with a beautiful view, overlooking many acres of peaceful, green land and trees. The staff treated me like royalty; and I treated them with respect as well. I was probably one of the best patients they ever had (aside from me ringing the hell out of that bell at all times of the night, and giving them a hard time about washing and sanitizing their hands!). I know they got a real kick out of me, because I certainly got kick out of them. They would come into my room trying to touch on me, and I would stop them in their tracks making them wash their hands, and put gloves on! I didn't want them touching me with their bare hands after fiddling with all of the other patients, and God only knows what else. I remember one assistant had the nerve to tell me, "Well you're the one the one with TB!"! I told her, "I don't care you're not touching me damn gloves on!". I reported her for giving me a hard time, and never had any more trouble afterwards.

The staff was used to dealing with mostly homeless, and uneducated people, but I wasn't having it. Some of them looked like they could have had the same thing we had; but they had a tough job that I'm sure didn't pay nearly what it should have.

There was one RN that came into my room one-day attempting to draw blood. I'm guessing he was inexperienced, and didn't know what he was doing. He stuck me in the PICC line to draw some blood, and forgot to close the vial. The next thing I knew, my blood went flying everywhere, missed me, and hit the wall! All he could say was, "Aww man, Royce! That was some tricky dicky stuff right there!" I looked at him and said, "WHAT?! What in the hell is tricky dicky?!". He said, "That blood flying everywhere was tricky dicky!" I told him he was crazy, and needed to go back to school or something! I can't make this stuff up; it was crazy funny even though I felt like my life was in danger most times. I told my wife about it, and to this very day we both still refer to him as "Tricky Dicky". A bit of advice for anyone being treated for any kind of illness right now, make SURE you get familiar with EVERY medication you are supposed to have. Know the names, colors, shapes, and even the quantities. Be sure to ask questions, and never trust or rely on the doctors and staff. Don't just take their word on things. They are human just like you, and subject to error.

Soon I was released as an outpatient to finish out my treatment at home. Since I was done with the injections, and had the PICC line removed, I only had oral medications left to complete. A caseworker was reassigned to come and administer my meds every single day, five days a week. On the weekends they entrusted me with the medications to take on my own. It is important to note, that I never stopped moving around or exercising during this process. Working out was my LIFE prior to my diagnosis. So, I walked every single day, no matter how bad it hurt. I kept on moving even when most people probably would have just stayed in bed. I was determined not to let this get the best of me. As long as I was still breathing, and able to walk, I was going to do my part to take care of myself, and let God take care of the rest. I would definitely feel a great deal of depression, and have mood swings a lot of times. So much so, that my wife called my doctor on me one day because she thought I had gone crazy! She just didn't understand the full effect the medications had on me. I was fine, but irritable, and needed to be left alone a lot of times. I was still crooked, and still couldn't feel that the treatment was working at this time; but I walk by faith, and not by sight. It's always mind over matter, and your perspective is everything in a situation like this one.

I felt like I was in a battle by myself because nobody in my family understood what I was going through. I'm so glad that I don't look like what I went through. I didn't then, and even more so now. It's a blessing, as well as a curse. I say it is also a take your health seriously when you're smiling all of the time. My family didn't come to San Antonio to visit me not even one time after I was admitted. They didn't even offer to help transport me back and forth once I couldn't drive anymore. I learned a harsh lesson during that time. If you're not broke down, slumped over, or decrepit, don't expect sympathy and consideration from people. I was barely making it, and still breaking my neck to go and visit my family when I would come to Houston on the weekends. They were beefing with my wife (and mad at me too in all honesty), and couldn't put their petty differences aside for the big picture. Despite all of the beef, I still wanted to maintain the relationship and spend time with them however I could.

I try not to hold on to things, but on some things, I have to speak. I recall about a year ago, my biological father was diagnosed with prostate cancer. Everyone was fluttered and up in a frenzy, ready to flock to his bedside. My sister was ready to hop on the road and drive all the way from Houston to Louisiana to see about him! She even tried to convince me to travel with her! We got into a huge argument, because I reminded her that she didn't travel one time to visit me in San Antonio. This guy was barely in our lives growing up, but she was more concerned about him than her own brother who's been here. I had a huge problem with that! I don't recap this to sound bitter, but to simply make a point. You know what she told me? "I didn't think it was that serious!". My mom and other family members all felt the same. I won't even lie to you;

heart to forgive them. I realized; life was too short to be falling out over something they could never understand.

At the end of my 2-year treatment plan, I was finally TB free! WHEW! GOD IS GOOD! Life now had a brand-new meaning. The wound in my back had completely healed, though I still had pain, and my spine still crooked. I still had my work cut out for me as far as recovery was concerned. It was going to take some time, and most of the hard part was done. However, I still had to face the detox from all of the rest of the medications, very similar to when I stopped all of the pain meds earlier on. I still experienced the same feelings of withdrawals that had me aching, and breaking out in cold sweats, but this round, I felt itchy as well to add to it. Honestly, I don't understand why anyone would want to willingly get addicted to drugs. I just couldn't voluntarily put myself through that kind of abuse. I don't even like having hangovers. The last hangover I had was New Year's Eve 2007; and it messed me up so bad I swore I would never do it again. Call me crazy, but feeling sick and being in pain just isn't my thing. I only deal with it when faced with the challenge. You really don't know what you are capable of until you are faced with a life-threatening situation. Your character, strength, and will power will either make you, or break you; but you cannot escape it. You just have to PUSH THROUGH, AND NEVER GIVE UP. That's the mentality of a winner; and I AM A WINNER.

A new journey was about to begin. I had to focus on putting my life back together. It was going obviously wasn't in the cards. It was all that I thought I knew though, so I had to figure out what my next career move was going to be. It was a harsh reality to face because I wanted it so bad, and gave it everything I had; but God had a different plan. I heard a saying once that said, "If you want to make God laugh, tell Him your plans". I imagine He was rolling on the floor laughing at me after listening to mine. Where do I go from here though? I have never considered myself to be a mediocre kind of guy, working a meaningless, mediocre job. I really didn't envision myself in a boring corporate America type job for the rest of my life. I stepped out of my comfort zone, and started tapping into different business ventures. It was a scary, but thrilling experience, because I didn't know where it was going to take me. I had a mortgage, and a high maintenance wife, so you know I had my work cut out for me when I made the decision not to return to corporate America. I made it work though, because I'm a hustler by blood. I always have a vision and a plan, and as long as you believe in yourself, you can make anything shake! You have to just plan your work, and then work your plan!

8

God's Blessing

So, time has passed, and now I am stronger, and much better. I was finally able to start jogging again, and my spine had finally straightened up. I now had a healthy weight to my 6"4 frame, and finally got my sexy back! YES, I SAID SEXY! I was BACK, and better than ever! That TB had me looking like a crackhead! All of those late-night chocolate doughnut calls in the hospital had finally paid off. I ate good then, and continued to eat even better after returning home. I never thought weight, as I was always relatively slim even prior to the TB. Now, the only downside was the numbness I still had in my feet, and I ended up needing glasses. The medications had caused a permanent loss of vision, though not as bad as what I had experienced earlier on during treatment. It's all good though, I will take these side effects any day over losing my life. It's so easy to complain when things don't turn out quite like you expect them to; but you have to know when to count your blessings. I always say, "IT'S ALL ABOUT THE LITTLE THINGS".

So, in the back of my mind, I could still hear that jerk of a doctor shattering my dreams saying I may never be able to have children. It nagged at me from that moment on, and even second guessing myself. I knew I wanted a family at some after battling with MDR Tuberculosis. I had a conversation with my wife regarding when she felt would be a good time to start trying for a baby. She was very reluctant, and felt we should wait a little longer until we were able to replenish our finances. Well, I was no longer with the waiting program after everything I had experienced. There's no time like the present, right?? Of course, it's always great to have more, but we were financially stable enough to provide for a child. You know how women can be though; EXTRA and over the top to say the least.

Unbeknownst to me, my wife had doubts about whether or not she could even get pregnant at this point. She was diagnosed with multiple fibroids four years prior, and had procrastinated on getting them removed. She was relying on her fibroids as a form of birth control. She would even joke occasionally saying that her eggs were dusty and she wasn't having any kids! Well I didn't find it all that funny and would be like, "Now why you wanna play with me?". That would start up a whole new argument because she thought it was a big joke, and I really wanted a baby! Somewhere along the way, our roles had gotten reversed. Normally, it's the woman who is adamant about having a child! I told her if she wouldn't give me any kids, I was OUT! I even told her that she tricked me into marrying her by promising me a couple of kids. She knew how badly I wanted a family, and she was taking it just a little too lightly for me at that moment. She wasn't there when the doctor insulted me with his pathetic expertise. To add to it, her doctor had even told her due to the positioning getting pregnant (she already knew this, which is why she wouldn't remove them). Now don't misunderstand me, I would never leave my wife for not being able to have children due to health issues; but she thought it was funny to tell me she didn't want to try for any altogether! She said she was too old and I had waited too long to put a ring on it, so she called herself trying to punish me. Boy, these women are something else! It was all out of love though, we would cut up and go in on each other, and then laugh about it all at the same time. We're crazy like that though, you have to know us to understand our madness.

My wife hadn't been on birth control in four years, and her doctor thought it was odd that she had not gotten pregnant considering. We were finally at a place where if it happened, it happened, and if it didn't, we were still okay with that (well my wife was, at least). Yet and still, you know doctors have a way of alarming you even when you feel like you're good. Dr. M. told us that if nothing happened within the next six months, she wanted to see my wife back in her office to check for fertility issues. Around late November or so, my wife was noticeably "late", when she was normally like clockwork. She was working out, but had gained a bump that she just couldn't seem to get rid of. I remember telling her to just go and get a couple of pregnancy tests, and put us both out of our misery. She was in strong denial, and must have taken around 6 tests before she finally came to terms that she was actually pregnant. I was through the ROOF with excitement! I knew that doctor everything, and in fact, don't know what they are doing half the time. I mean think about it, most times when you go to the doctor, you are telling them what is wrong or what you think is wrong, and they check to see if you are correct about your own diagnosis! They probably search symptoms on Google just like the rest of us; but they hit the books and put in the work in order to get the big bucks. No disrespect to the doctors out there. I know they mean well because I was blessed with a team that finally came through for me; but I didn't appreciate that one TB back specialist handling me in the way that he did. I literally contemplated driving back to San Antonio to shove our ultrasound pictures in his face. God showed up for me in a big way, and I couldn't have planned a better Christmas gift because this was worth more than any money could buy.

This process didn't go easy though, and I was used to the bad following the good. We were on eggshells the entire pregnancy, due to the fibroids putting my wife at a huge risk. We would have to attend her regular appointments, as well as see the high-risk OB/GYN. We were really on eggshells thinking our baby would have growth issues because of the fibroids. All in all, the pregnancy went cautious, but well.

The day finally came when our baby boy made his debut! After a gruesome labor and delivery, he had finally arrived weighing in at a healthy 8 pounds and 5ounces! WON'T HE DO IT?!?! All I needed was faith the size of a mustard seed, and God delivered. Becoming a father has been far. Sometimes you have to block out all negativity in order to receive God's promises. I was strong and determined enough not to let man determine my fate.

9

The Million Dollar Man

If you had asked me five years ago where I would be right about now, I probably would have said somewhere overseas playing professional basketball, or something along those lines. I never would have imagined in a million years that I would be an MDR Tuberculosis survivor, married with a son, and now sharing my story with the world. I like to refer to myself as the "Million Dollar Man". Is it due to what's in my bank account, per se? Absolutely not (YET)! I'm the Million Dollar Man because of the entire treatment and care that I received throughout my journey. I was blessed to receive medications for every ache and pain, multiple MRI's, free dental work, countless specialist appointments, rehabilitation, group therapy and the list goes on. Let's not forget, room and board free of charge, and all the food and snacks that I could stand. This was not a cheap bill by far. Listen up guys, I'm going to go deep for a bit so stay with me. We place a lot of value of money and material things; but the real wealth is a clean slate of health. Think about it, you can have a billion dollars in your bank account, but how will it serve you once you're in the grave? Better yet, how much of that can you enjoy if you're gravely ill and bed ridden, without the activities of your limbs? HEALTH is wealth. Period. As long as you are healthy and strong enough to get out of bed, you are blessed and have the power to live your best life. You can't spend money from the grave. Once your time is up, it's up.

Battling MDR Tuberculosis took courage, determination, and will power. I strongly believe that my athletic background and competitive mentality contributed to me successfully conquering this illness. This process is not for the weak or the faint at heart, and believe it or not, is quite comparable to battling cancer and chemotherapy. Research has shown that about a third of the world's population (approximately two billion) is diagnosed with TB. The media doesn't but you can catch it much faster than HIV and cancer because it is airborne. It is a public threat and they probably don't want to alarm people. When someone infected around you openly coughs, sneezes, laughs, sings, or etc., their bacteria is released into the air. If you come along and breathe it in by chance, you will catch it also. Much like cancer, if TB goes untreated, it can spread throughout your body, and kill you. It is also contagious in many cases, and it can spread very rapidly to other people around you. TB is preventable and treatable (in most cases), but since I had MDR, my case was a bit more dangerous and complicated. My family and friends looked at me like 'awww, poor Royce', when they really should have been hauling ass to get tested. A TB screening should be mandatory for everyone at least twice a year, and that's minimum. I urge you all to incorporate TB screenings into your annual check-ups (and more frequent than that if possible). People always think it can't or won't happen to them, but I'm a living testimony that it can, and it DID.

Basketball or no basketball, I am a champion, and I am a survivor. I have proven to myself through this gruesome experience of TB, that my game is much stronger than on the basketball court. I'm in the game now called LIFE; and I'm winning at all costs through grind, grit, and tenacity! I had to dig deep, and go to a mental dimension that I had never gone before. To God be the Glory for the things HE has done!

waiting list for treatment as soon as I was diagnosed. I don't know how, and I don't know why; but God saw fit for me to be in that number. The treatment and resources that were accessible to me were invaluable, and certainly out of my budget! I want to take the time to thank Dr. K. and her team, the entire nursing staff, the research analysts, the cooks, and all of the other hospital staff that accommodated me, and all of the other patients that have been treated (and still being treated). Thank you, guys, for interrupting my sleep throughout the day and night, because it was all for the greater good. To everyone who is battling any kind of illness, DON'T GIVE UP! Stay close to those who are suffering with you. Find comfort and solace in one another, because only they can relate to what you are feeling and going through.

Stay positive, and never stop moving no matter how difficult it may be. Find a happy place in the midst of your storm, and do little things that will bring you a smile. If it's no more than reading a book, or sitting in a place enjoying a peaceful scenery. Always remember, discomfort is temporary; but if you give up, it can last a lifetime.

Acknowledgements

I would like to thank God first and foremost, for bringing me through this journey, and even giving me the courage to open up my life and share it with people all over the world. I don't believe He took me through this experience for me to selfishly keep it to myself. I also want to thank my beautiful wife, for standing by me, and working tirelessly with me on this special project near and dear to my heart. I want to thank God for my adorable, handsome, rambunctious little boy who was also here every step of the way trying to destroy the computer and material every chance he got (LOL)!

I want give a shout out to my family who have impacted my life and story a great deal, and shaped me into the man that I am today. A HUGE thanks to the doctors and staff at TCID and the entire TB organization, who cared for me, provided a cure, and nursed me back to WEALTH! You guys will forever hold a special place in my heart. I pray that you will continue to create success stories such as mine, and bring TB awareness to people all over the world.

Last, but not least, a special thanks in advance to everyone who supports this project, and inspired enough to share it with others. It is my greatest hope that we can collectively bring awareness and prevention to TB, so that more lives are saved. Remember, there is no COMMUNITY, without UNITY. God Bless!

Royce L. Gaye

Million Dollar Man : Surviving Tuberculosis

Copyright © 2018 by Royce Gaye

Published by RLG's

For information contact :

royce_gaye@yahoo.com

Book and Cover photo/design by Elle Gaye